# Pebbles, Eggs and the Fence

# 鹅卵石、鸡蛋和栅栏

# Pebbles, Eggs and the Fence
# 鹅卵石、鸡蛋和栅栏

## A Collection of Poetry from Central Asia
## 中亚诗歌集

Ardakh Nurgaz

translated by

Ouyang Yu 欧阳昱

PUNCHER & WATTMANN

First published in 2021
Published by Puncher and Wattmann
PO Box 279
Waratah NSW 2298

http://www.puncherandwattmann.com
puncherandwattmann@bigpond.com

NATIONAL
LIBRARY
OF AUSTRALIA

A catalogue entry for this book is available from the National Library of Australia.

ISBN      9781925780697

Printed by Lightning Source International

# Contents

阿尔达克·努尔哈兹 —— 哈萨克诗人，剧作家，批评家。1972 年生，1995 年大学毕业，1991 年开始发表作品。2006 —— 2008 年任哈萨克斯坦《外国文学报》主编。出版诗集《伪自由书》(2009 年)，《蜂鸟集》(汉语、哈语，2012 年)，《精确与纯净》(英语，汉语、哈语，2014 年)，《A Garden of Trees and Other Poems》(英语，2017 年)，评论集《哈萨克现代诗歌论》(2010 年)，《认识与批评》(2018 年) 和短篇小说集《横与点》(2010 年)，等。诗歌作品英语，俄语，汉语等发表。剧作《我，我谁也不是》(2017 年) 获得《Pyx》国际文学评论奖剧作一等奖。

Ardakh Nurgaz is a Kazakh poet, essayist, dramaturge and critic, born in 1972. He graduated from university in 1995, and began publishing work in 1991. From 2006 to 2008, he was editor-in-chief of *Foreign Literatures*, a bi-monthly in Kazakhstan. He has published such poetry collections as *A Book of Pseudo Freedoms* (2009) and *A Collection of Humming Birds* (in Chinese and Kazakh, 2012). Nurgaz has also published a collection of literary criticism, *On Modern Kazakh Poetry* (2010) and a collection of short fiction, *Tanym mentalgam (Horizontal Strokes and Dots)* (2018). His play, titled 'I, I am Nobody', won the first place for drama in the first Pyx (Soul) International Literary Prize.

# 城市中的河流

小河饶流
像穿透历史的血脉
流过城市的大街小巷
河中流躺着泡摸，色料，泥巴和垃圾
看着河水
好想遇见五十年前的
父亲的童年
他也在笑，像你
看着太阳，眯着眼睛
很像你，望眼河水
虽然他的小纸船没有漂向远处
身影却在流淌
可你是见不到他的
你的孩子也不玩小纸船
她在水泥地上玩
木桥早就不见了
不要找了
现在是一座石桥
石桥上虽然见不到悬挂的人头
还是要快一点儿过
不然，不是马车
汽车会把你撞到

# The River in the City

The little river, meandering, runs
Like a vein of history
Through streets or lanes of the city
In the river lie soaked pita bread, coloring material, mud and trash
As I look at the river
I feel as if I had met Father 50 years ago
In his childhood
He is smiling, like you
Looking at the sun, his eyes narrowed
Like you, eyeing the river
Although his little paper boat has not drifted far
His shadow keeps flowing
Still, you can't see him
And your daughter is not playing with the paper boat
She is playing on the cement ground
The wooden bridge long gone
No point looking for it
There is a stone bridge now
Even though you won't see human heads hanging on it
You have to be quick
Or else cars, not horse-drawn
Carriages will hit you

# 阴影

影子占据门口
影子…
孔雀般蝴蝶的眼睛
邮递送来的信封上的地址
落叶中瞧见了你的面孔
锁子上沾者断钥匙的锈
是你的容貌？
蚊子飞过
留下看不见得踪迹
你的脚印
我把手往油墨里伸
你给自己画了个绕圈

# The Shadow

The shadow is occupying the doorway

The shadow...

The eyes of the butterfly like a peacock

The address on the envelope delivered by the postman

In the fallen leaves, your face is seen

The keyhole stained with the rust of the broken key

Or are those your facial features?

When a mosquito flies

It leaves invisible traces

Your footsteps

I put my hand in the printing ink

You draw a circle around yourself

# 耶路撒冷

时间消失在钟里
生命在颤抖
一时的恐惧和永恒之间
或在空中
不，不是的！
有人在上，有人在下的公共汽车上
他撕开了死神的面具
一滴血像雪花似的飘开
冬天的烟雾弹击中了要害

一个小生命的死亡
引来另一个小生命的终结
活亡灵游荡的大街上
并不响起
奔向深渊世纪的懊悔
电视屏幕上
尽是些挥霍昨天者的嘶叫声
和明天的面无全废的脸
心碎的如滴石泪水的悲歌
你也是屏息呼吸
盯视屏幕上的黑暗
并黑暗淹没的六十亿沉默者的一分子

追随自己声音飞翔的苍蝇
撞上镜子
改变了方向
一时停顿的世界中
忽然，梦中惊醒
撞进了岩石般的命运

# Jerusalem

Time has disappeared in the clock
Life trembling
Between momentary fear and eternity
Or in the air
No, not right!
On board the public bus, someone above and someone below
He tears open the mask of Death
A drop of blood, drifting off, like a snow flake
The smoke grenade of winter hitting home

The death of a small life
Leads to the termination of another
On a street where dead souls, alive, are roaming
No regret sounds
That rushes towards the abyss century
On TV screen
There are all those yowling who have squandered yesterday
And those featureless faces of tomorrow
Sad songs of broken heart pieces, like tears dripping from the stone
You, too, holding your breath
Watch the darkness on the screen
An element of the 6 billion silent, drowned by the dark

The fly that flies following its own sound
Hits the mirror
And changes its direction
In a world, momentarily suspended
The dream, suddenly waking up in surprise
Crashes into the fate like a rock

# 一朵花

我栽上一朵花，献送给太阳
燃烧的太阳
很明亮
永远陪伴着孤独
黑暗像群鸟似的飞走

豪饮太阳的光辉
我的心脏也暴跳
她也在一紧，一松
像点亮的烛火
奔向对岸的浪花

太阳献给花朵
自己永不凋谢的色
我的心也花瓣似的方开
鲜艳的像一滴血

# A Flower

I planted a flower, to offer to the sun
The burning sun
Very bright
Always accompanying loneliness
Darkness flying away, like birds

Drinking the brilliance of the sun to my heart's content
I feel my heart is beating violently
Tightening, and loosening up
Like a candle, just lit

Flowers of wave rushing to the other shore

The sun offered to the flower
Its own never-fading colours
My heart also opens, the way the petal of a flower does
Vividly fresh, like a drop of blood

# 沉默

拉下夜的帘子的手
在笑
看着光
瓶子中喘不过气的是
一片云——
光

穿过黑夜眼珠的箭
留下
白色的印烙
窗外
流星划过夜幕

# Silence

The hand that pulled down the shutters of the night
Is laughing
Looking at the light
What is breathless in the bottle is
A spread of cloud—
Light

The arrow, going through the eyeballs of the dark night
Has left
White branding marks
Outside the window
A meteor is flitting across the screen of the night

# 鸟

我醒来时，我的木摇篮在摇晃
慢慢的，在风中摇晃

沉没在心底的铃铛声中
浮现出千年的幽灵
我跟崔着巡夜人手中的烛光
一只飞剑似的天鹅
朝黑色天空的万丈深渊飞去
耳旁，风在呼唤，
扑过来的是消逝在大漠中的琴音
骆驼崽的衰叫声和干湖的沉思

我睁开眼睛
一只小鸟飞过来
鸟在谛鸣：
" 胡木是你的母亲
你叫贺甫恰克 "*

---

* 贺甫恰克 — 中亚民族之一，传说中说贺甫恰克人是树生出来的。

# The Bird

When I woke up, my wooden cradle was rocking
Slowly, in the wind

Sinking into the ringing of the bell at the bottom of my heart
As a ghost of thousand years emerged
I was following the candle in the hand of a night watchman
When a sword-like swan
Flew towards the abyss of the black skies
At my ears, the wind was calling
What was rushing towards me was the sound of a qin that had disappeared
in the great desert*
The sad cries of camelets and the deep thoughts of a dry lake

When I opened my eyes
A bird came flying over
Saying as it chirped:
'The walnut tree is your mother
and your name is Kipchaks'**

---

* 'Qin' is a musical instrument.
** Kipchaks are one of the ethnic races in Central Asia. Legend has it that they were born out of a tree.

# 林园私语

林园很寂静，并不相广场
世界尽头的那蓝色地平线
没有喧哗，没有音乐，没有笑声
和石街上传出的脚步声
没有摧毁后又重建的纪念碑
也不会听到林中夜莺的白日鸣谛

满地秋色的落叶在脚下沉没
并根着脚趾一起齐舞
散发着苔藓和腐木的香气
心潮独芳，
你在潮湿的暗流中挺胸
喧哗的阴影在离开
头顶上的呐喊者
假笑者和潜意志中的撒谎者在变脸

你停住脚步，落叶在私语
一只蚂蚁或一只蚯蚓的行军
也使你心醉
微风吹拂着河边的青草，火香草
带来遥远的记忆
你一定会想起祖先的
"有火香草，就有救"那一句
在河边吮吸静和火香草
默默流失的暗笑的时间中
感觉到自己水中的影子在渐渐黯淡
是的，太阳在落下
很优伤

# Private Language in a Woodland

Very quiet, the woodland does not resemble a square
On the blue horizon at the end of the world
There's no noise, no music, no laughter
No footsteps from the stone street
No monuments rebuilt after destruction
No daylight singing of a nightingale that one could hear


The fallen leaves of autumn, covering and colouring the ground, are
sinking under foot
And dancing with the toes
Fragrances, mixed with moss and rotten wood
Scenting, alone, the waves of heart
You throw your shoulders back, in the hidden currents of moisture
As the uproarious shadows are leaving
Above my head, the shouters
The false smilers and the liers in the subconscious are changing faces


You stop in your tracks, the fallen leaves engaged in a private language
The marching of an ant or a worm
Intoxicates you
The breeze is blowing across the green grass on the riverbanks, and the fire-
fragrant grass
Has brought in distant memories
Surely, you'll remember the remark
Our ancestors said, 'There is salvation if there is fire-fragrant grass'
By the river, as I suck the stillness and the fire-fragrant grass
In the hidden laughter time that is quietly flowing and losing
I feel that my own shadow in the water is, little by little, darkening
Yes, when the sun sets
It is very sad

# 画

合上眼睛
也许不是另一次迷失

慢慢升起的朝霞中
参出一条路
他挽起腰来
捡到了一把钥匙
落日似的火炭
手掌上留下了不灭的伤疤
门缝撕开
有人递给他一只白玫瑰

升起的太阳在天空中
猛烈燃烧
手中留下的是花瓣似的烙印
紧闭的门后面是
茫茫沙丘
有一颗树
树上到挂着一个死的小鸟

# The Painting

Eyes closed
It may not be another loss

In the morning glow that slowly rises
A road is impeached
He, bent double
Picks up a bunch of keys
The burning charcoal, like the setting sun
Scars, undistinguishable, left on the palm
The crack in the door torn open
Someone gives him a white rose

The risen sun in the sky
Fiercely burning
What is left on the hand is a mark that resembles a petal
And behind the closed door is
A vastness of sand dunes
There is a tree
On which a dead bird is hanging

# 雨

蒙蒙细雨
辟盖路面的落叶被雨滴
击鼓，不知
是你的眼泪
雨中，送别你已经远去的身影
我的心
被雨水参透的翅膀似的
孤独地归来

到处是积水残叶
脚底下就有一篇
踩着的却不是树叶
树叶用一生的激情倾泻
手掌中有一只蝴蝶
不飞，不动
沉消在自己的夜中

雨，沉默

# The Rain

A fine drizzle

Fallen leaves, covering the road surfaces, drummed

By its drops, not sure if they are

Your tears

In the rain, seeing you off as you are furthering away

My heart

Like a feather, drenched in rainwater

Returns alone

Puddles and tattered leaves everywhere

There is one underfoot

But what is being treaded upon is not a leaf

The leaves pour, with the passion of a lifetime

A butterfly on the palm

Not flying, not moving

Sinking into its own night

The rain, silence

# 观望

手中滑落
丢失了
我凝视水面
水中影子在观我
向我舒开胸怀
像亲吻蜜蜂的花朵
微尘起舞，花瓣放飞
我抬起头来望天
是的，他在观我

# Watching

Slipping out of hand

Getting lost

I gaze at the water

The shadow in the water is watching me

Opening its heart to me

Like a flower that kisses the bees

Dust dances, flowers in flight

I look up at the sky

Yes, he is looking at me

# 蛋

从大街回到家
孩子在门口迎接我
世界是一个圆圆的蛋
曾经一个朋友就这么说过

街上一群人突然现身
强行抵制另一些人
看着讲述谜语者自告答案似的
我们彼此无知相对

一瞬间，脚一起一落
树上的小鸟侧身跳到另一支树枝
手持警棍的警察
向街对面的人大喊大叫

街面到处是残叶
树叶跟着脚步跃起
曲线上的那一个音符
不知什么时候丢失

用石头撞击石头
一身粉碎
这是我知道的
谁来告诉我真谛
为什么用蛋来碰石头
还是蛋结下了被碰石头的缘？！

# Egg

Back home from the street
My kid welcomes me at the door
The world is a round egg
A friend once told me

A crowd of people suddenly emerges on the street
Forcibly resisting a number of others
Looking at the riddle-teller seemingly offering his answer
We face one another, no idea

In an instant, the foot lifts and falls
A bird, in a tree, turning around, leaps to another branch
The police, batons in hand
Are yelling at the people on the street

Broken leaves everywhere on the street
That jump with footsteps
The musical note on the curve
Is lost one knows not when

Stones smash into stones
All shattered
That much I know
Who's there to tell me the truth
Why smash the eggs against the stones
Or is it something serendipitous?!

# 雪地

失忆的雪覆盖着大地
白色的原野上
留下的是可辨认的足迹
路在寻找自己的尽头
好似冲上手指头的那一瞬间

雪飘然落下
沉默的箱子无声地打开
并关上
好像用清晰含义被填满
锁住昨日和当下的时间

望着原野

我叫了一声
开始散开的云间
兜着玩的蓝天在看
白雪，欲望，阴影和寂静下
洁白的路在藏而不露的废墟上
缓缓远行

# Snowfield

Snow, whose memory is lost, has covered the land
The white open country
Is left with traceable footsteps
The road, in the instant it rushes towards the finger
Is looking for its end

The snow, floating, falls
The suitcase, silent, opens up
And closes
As if it were filled with clear meaning
Locking up the time of yesterday and the present

Watching the plain

I give a yell
In the clouds that are beginning to disperse
The sky, playful, is watching
Below the white snow, desire, shadows and quietness
A clean and white road, on the hidden rubble
Slowly, goes into the distance

# 卵石

几棵白杨树之后
是树林
夜已来到林中
带一批奔马的小骑手
骑马穿过小河
马蹄声哗然响起
惊吓的小鸟从树上飞去
水中跳出来的小石头
掉在我跟前，我捡起黑色石头
激流涛就的卵石很像我的眼珠
我看着石头寻找往事的记忆
那马蹄似的坚硬和不灭的毅力…
骑马的小孩已走到林中
消失了
留下的是钟声般的黑夜

# Pebbles

Behind a number of white poplars

Is the woods

Where the night has arrived

Taking a group of young riders on horseback

Across a small river

The sound of hoofbeating

And a scared tiny bird that flies off the tree

The small stones that jump out of the water

Fall in front of me before I pick up a black one

The pebbles, cast by the rapids, resemble my eyeballs

I look at them for a memory of the past

The hardness and the undying fortitude, like the hooves...

The kid riders have walked into the woods

And disappeared

Leaving the dark night, like the sound of the bell

# 棚栏

雪和光
相遇
带来的是黑暗
我闭着眼睛
沉默

手中握着一捏土，一粒麦子，一朵玫瑰
在血迹斑斑的广场上
花是从你的手中接过来
想把它擦在自己窗前的花瓶上

夏日出巢的小鸟
在冬日的寒冷下，雪地上
小心地分享食物
稚嫩的羽线上
显露出冬日的阳光

白纸上留下的一个小迹
白雪中无义露出来的一个印
用白布裹起来的大地
手指头的那微列的一动

手中握着一粒麦子，一捏土
我把它撒在雪地上
跨出一步 —
推倒沉默的棚栏
大地因该祥有她自己的彦色

# The Fence

When snow and light
Meet
They bring in darkness
I close my eyes and go
Silent

Grabbing hold of a pinch of soil, a grain of wheat, a rose
On the blood-stained square
The flower, received from your hand
Likes to plant it inside the vase before its own window

The little bird, out of its nest on a summer day
In the wintry cold and on the snow
Is, carefully, sharing the food
Its tender feather lines
Showing the sunshine of a winter day

A small trace, left on the white paper
A seal, unintentionally revealed in the white snow
The land, wrapped up with a white cloth
A slight movement at the tip of a finger

Grabbing hold of a grain of wheat, a pinch of soil
I chuck it onto the snow
As I step out—
Pushing the silent fence down
The land needs to have its own colours

# 精确与纯净

（献给 Wislawa Szymborska）

沿着漆黑，无底的井
落下的石头似的
房间
我无法从嘴唇道出你去了
虽说面向你曙光般亲切的容貌
已开起天堂的门

那照在喧哗世界的
阳光似的诗篇
曾穿透
帝国无边的围墙
我知道
你是不会恐惧黑暗的
你是否沿着自己的足迹
离开了哪个唯一的岛
我喉咙中的献给你的诗句
在无声的海中漫游

有时我们把精确叫作纯净
林中起风，万叶飘浮
从中阴影起身
混乱的世界失去平衡时
你载下了面具
手掌心中飞出来一只
北方的蜂鸟

# Pure and Accurate

(For Wislawa Szymborska)

Along the black, bottomless well
The room
Like a fallen stone
I found it impossible to voice you
Although the gate of heaven had opened
To your intimate features like the first light of the day

The poem, like sunshine
That had shone on the noisy world
Had penetrated
The boundless wall of the empire
I know
You won't fear darkness
And I wonder if you have left the sole island
Along your own footsteps
Poems, for you, in my throat
Are wandering in the soundless sea

Sometimes we call accuracy purity
The wind is up in the forest and leaves are drifting
Dark shadows are rising amidst them
When the confused world is losing its balance
You remove your mask
As a humming bird from the north
Is flying out of the heart of the palm

# 幻觉

血腥冲天的大院中
两个刽子手把斧头阁在一边
在下棋
开始走步的婴儿在追
翅膀烧伤而无法高飞的蝴蝶
院墙外
有人围着斗殴的公鸡
摔帽子，大喊大叫
塔尖上无影的弯月经历苍苍
而忧伤
为早晨的祷告而醒来的人们
开始站队
看护人还未到的墓地旁
帮着一只无耳朵和尾巴的狗
嚎叫声仅次于凄凉的哭声

# Illusion

In the big courtyard where blood was rushing to high heaven

Two butchers, with their axes left to the side

Were playing chess

The toddler, who had just began walking, was chasing

A butterfly, with wings burnt, that could not fly high

Outside

There were people encircling the fighting cocks

Who threw their hats and yelled

The curved moon, shadowless, at the tip of the tower, was much experienced

And sad

People who had woken for the morning prayer

Began queuing up

The keeper had not yet arrived at the graveyard

He was helping a dog without ears or tail

Whose howling was second only to the forlorn weeping

# 第 492 次核爆炸

在黄昏，彼夜色笼罩的西方
突然
开设升起太阳
以前也见过此理的光
我们震惊，放弃玩捉谜藏
先害怕，后无比的兴奋起来

从新开始捉谜藏以前
我向
黑暗中升起
并把黑暗推倒半天空
而后彼黑暗逐渐吞噬的光
看了一眼
最后的几线白色在头顶上消失

传来一声，妈妈喊我回家
我挥着手说："告别了，光！"
可万万没有想到，
这次不是我而是光在说：
"告别了！"

# The 492nd Nuclear Explosion

At dusk, in the west, shrouded by the night
The sun, suddenly
Begins to rise
I used to see such a light before
When we were so shocked we gave up on playing hide and seek
First afraid, then incredibly excited

As I began on my new hide and seek
I rose
Towards darkness
As I pushed down half the dark sky
Before I took a glance
At the last few lights, gradually eaten up by the dark
Disappeared over my head

Mom's call came, asking me home
As I waved and said, "Farewell, Light!"
Little did I expect that
This time round it's the light, not I, that said:
"Farewell!"

# 灵魂

你是谁？
从何而来，何处去
关起一扇门，大开另一扇门
你是否找到自己一直寻找的栖居地
我曾感觉到你在我手中的笔尖停留一时
仿佛阳光层层参透蜻蜓翅膀似的
一想到你，我的心如风吹得灯芯
你是谁的恩惠？
为何冰雪君临风暴笼罩的没有尽头的路途上夜行
为何总是稳藏在祷告和钟声中
为何窝巢在我的心中
无法承受你那无比的沉重是
我折断双翅的鸟儿似的旋转
我抬起头，你是母亲的吻
悲伤时，你是远处大海骚动的波涛
惊惶时，你是我梦得天空中突然现身的白色的云
惋惜时，你是镜中身影追捕昏暗的延伸
我开始奔跑，你是我胸膛上起舞的风
我开始旋转，你是我心灵中冒燃浮起的音乐
是我黑暗中升起的无法避开的阶梯
你是我耳中奏鸣的小鸟
张开双掌，你是我禁不住涌上眼窝的泪水
为什么对我如此地感慨
你，你是谁？

# Soul

Who are you?

Where are you from and where are you going?

Close one door and keep another wide open

Can you find the resting place you have been looking for?

I once had the feeling that the tip of your pen stayed in my hand for a while

Like the sunshine that showed through the overlapping wings of the
dragon flies

At the thought of you, my heart, like a lampwick, was blown by the wind

Whose boon are you?

Why do the ice and snow reign over the night travel on an endless road
shrouded in a storm

Why always hide in the sound of prayers and the bell

Why always make a nest in my heart

Unable to take your unmatched heaviness

I gyrate the way a bird does, with its broken wings

When I raise my head, you are Mother's kiss

When I grow sad, you are waves surging in the distant sea

When I panic, you are the white cloud that suddenly appears in the sky of
my dream

When I feel sorry, you are an extension of yourself in the mirror chasing
after darkness

When I begin running you are the wind that dances on my chest

And when I gyrate, you are the music that emerges in my heart

The staircase, unavoidable, that rises in my darkness

You are a little bird that sings in my ears

With your palms spread, you are tears that come to my eyes

Why are you so generous towards me

You, who are you?

# 两烛火

"死亡开花了，只开一次， / 开得不像它自己"
　　　　　　－保罗·策兰

夜，原野
木柴在燃烧
林立的赤焰
在向灰暗喷吐

黑夜无限
可我们不是孤独的
各自在火的一旁
感觉到彼此的存在

我望着火势
他拿着火柴根
每次打磨
火柴激烈地燃烧
燃烧后就是熄灭

他把烧了一半的火柴根
撂掉一边
从新拿一只
黑夜抵近的脚步声似的
蟋蟀在近处谛叫

我看着他的脸
想说：多么短暂的一丝光
可还是没有说出来

# Two Candle Fires

"Death in flower, only for once / Not like itself"
        — Paul Celan


Night, the steppe
The firewood burning
The red flames, like a woods
Spitting into the grey darkness

The dark night unlimited
But we are not lonely
As we sit on either side of the fire
Conscious of each other's presence

I watching the momentum of the fire
He holding a matchstick
Each time he strikes it
The matchfiercely burns
Before it burns out

He chucks the half-burnt stick
To one side
And picks up another one
The dark night approaches in audible footsteps
The crickets are chirping nearby

I look at his face
I want to say· what a transitory light
But before I can say it

他把烧完的柴根扔进火堆中
站起身，走到一旁
面对着黑夜

"一丝光"
望着燃烧中的两烛火
我在沉思

He chucks the burnt stick into the fire

Stands up and walks to one side

Facing the dark night

"A light"

Watching the two candle fires that are burning

I fall into a deep reverie

# 地铁

父亲和儿子
在地铁的入口处
生活在继续

光和阴
儿子着急地想走进地铁
父亲想尽量地停留在阳光中

一丝光阴
生命在奔驰
想把父亲带出另一个入口处

顷刻间的停留
儿子虽然带着父亲离开
还是会留下一个意念

肩并肩的行程
一个在奔跑
另一个在停留

生命就是你怎么敲也无法开启的
迷宫门

# In the Subway

The son and the father
At the entrance to the subway
Life goes on

Ti and me
The son wants to hurry into the subway
The father wants to stay as long as possible in the sun

A streak of ti-me
Life is galloping
Intending to take the father into another entrance

An instant stop
Even though the son will leave with his father
A thought will be left behind

A journey shoulder to shoulder
One is running
And the other, staying

Life is the entrance to a labyrinth
That you have no way of opening however hard you knock on it

# 有人在夜下等车

沉默，在一次临近
是的，你的手指握在我的手心上

演员们互换面具
把手中的剑仍在了舞台上
最后一刻
观众起身
响起暴雨般的鼓掌声

序幕落下
后台上听得出另一种脚步声
观众在离席

戏刚刚开始
误以为达到目的地而搞错下车的人
在夜中黑影似的在路边招手等车
从麦地起飞的鸟群风中乌云搬旋转着后
又回到了原处
巨浪般漂浮的麦田上唯一静止的是
一只高高在上的木偶

# Someone is waiting for the bus under the night

Silence that approaches once again
Yes, your fingers held in the heart of my hand

The actors are swapping their masks
Throwing down their swords on the stage
In the last minute
The audience stand up
As a storm of applause rises

As the curtain falls
Footsteps, of another kind, become audible on the back stage
As the audience are leaving

The play has only just begun
The one who disembarks on a wrong destination
Is waiting for the bus, waving like a shadow by the roadside
The flock of birds that takes flight from behind the wheat-field, like clouds
                                                              in the wind
Have returned to where they were
The only thing that keeps still, high up
Is the wooden puppet floating above the field, like a huge wave

# 语言

帝国时期留下的建筑物上的旗帜凝重
感觉到从远方逼近的暴风雨在到来
节日后的广场人无而沉寂
是深水中掠过的潜水者的影子似的

喇叭花茎上停留的岁月
在深夜开花
随河流倒向飞奔的日子
于随流星远去

火柴棍爆燃，历史
白纸上的黑点突然被点亮
黑夜中的黑猫在倾听

我把自己的梦捏成一团后
撕碎成碎片洒向空中
一生为代价伴奏的曲目
终于被奏完似的停下
伸出手掌
落下的是从高处的深渊中飘下来的雪

语言
旋转中沿着圈行驶的旋风
在追随遗忘
语言
请停留片刻
让光照亮内心的黑暗

# Language

The flag is heavy, above the building left from the time of empire
One feels that the storm, forging ahead from a distance, is arriving
The square after the festival is deserted and quiet
Resembling the shadow of a diver that flits through the depths of water

Years stopped on the stems of the morning glory
Burst into flowers deep at night
Days that rush backwards
Are gone with the meteors

The matchsticks crackle into flames, history
Black spots, on the white paper, are suddenly lit up
And a black cat is listening, in the dark night

When I roll my dream into a ball in my fist
I scatter the shreds into the sky
An accompanied number, at the expense of a life
Eventually comes to an end, as if played out
When the hand is held forth
What falls is the snow, from the abyss on high

Language
A whirlwind, turning,that drives around a circle
Is chasing after memory
Language
Please stop a minute
And let the light shine on the darkness of the heart

# 窗户

新建的房子有很多窗户
从中有两个是相对的
不知怎么，每次面对窗户我有个感觉另一个在背后盯着我看
好像街上走过去的老人和孩子似的
因此我喜欢这两扇窗户
两扇窗户一个面向东方，另一个面向西方
从一个窗户看到黎明时的紫光，另一扇看到的是落日的暗淡
老人牵着小孩，还是小孩在牵着老人
我感觉到他们在彼此牵着手走
一扇窗户是黑暗，另一扇便是蜡烛的光芒
是的，他们是牵着手的一对
一切由你，怎么看
虽然没有足迹，可路还是明显的

# The window

The newly built house has many windows
Two of which are opposite each other
For some reason, I always get the feeling that someone is staring at me from
behind
When I face the window
Like the old man and his kid who walk down the street
For this reason, I like these two windows
One window faces east, and the other, west
From one I can see the purple light of the dawn, and from the other, the
darkening setting-sun
Is the old man leading his kid, or the kid the old man?
My feeling is that they are holding each other's hand
One window is darkness, and the other, the light of a candle
Yes, they are a pair, hand in hand
It's all up to you how you look at it
No footsteps there are but the road is apparent

# 悬崖上的风

"如果我身体上能感到似乎自己头顶洞开，我就知道那是诗"
                                              —E·狄金森

I

终于跨出自己一步，原野
内与外并立，沉浮无限的空间
一处是天眼，漩涡的感应

另一处是路
（白纸上的词逐渐沉没似的诗句在暗淡）
比黑夜更黑的足迹在召唤

叶子早已凋零的枯枝上
窝着几只黑鸟
佛晓前的黑暗中树顶开始骚动
黑鸟来回飞掠
雪地上到处是漂浮不定的阴影

突然推开窗户似的
挣开眼睛
疯狂的太阳底下站着几位
中间冷笑的就是那一位
充满爱的一滴光造就的尘世
从泥土欲试发芽，

# Wind on the Cliff

If I feel physically as if the top of my head were taken off, I know that is poetry.
    — Emily Dickinson


I


I have, finally, stepped out of myself, the plain
Its inside and outside in parallel, the space, sinking and floating, infinitely
One spot being the eye of the sky, the sensation of the vortex

The other being the road
(words on the white paper gradually sink, it seems, as poetic lines dim)
Footsteps, darker than the dark night, are calling

Leaves long withered on the dry branches
Nesting a few black birds
In the darkness before dawn, the crown of the trees begins to stir
Where the black birds flit, to and fro
On the snow, there are shady shadows adrift everywhere

The window is suddenly pushed open
And the eyes, too, open themselves
The beings* are standing under the crazy sun
The one with a cold smile is the one
The dusty world, created by a dropful of love
Is trying to bud, from the earth

---

\*   6 forms in human life, such as youth, age, beauty, sickness, ugliness, hypocrisy and desire.
Translator's note: This poem, originally written in Kazakh language and translated into
Chinese by the poet's wife, Gulnar Ahan, was translated into English from its Chinese version.

黑暗中的黑跟着起步飞来

荒废的田野被秋天蔓延的野火吞蚀
从历史跳出来的一群孩子在街上
踢着向日葵在喧闹

骰子掷过去，翻滚出的路
走到了岩石脚下
黎明时我从空无的池塘中
游出水面似的醒来

石墙出现的裂缝间
风透过来
习惯生活在手掌心中的人们
暴露在公海上
从垃圾箱悠悠升起的浓烟
掩盖了过山坡的游牧者
爬到时间天平上的人们
在深深的眼窝可以装几升土

参入到酒中的毒
也有属于它的时针
如果钟声不按时震响
玫瑰的花瓣是不会芬芳的

近处是草原，远处是海
快要梦断了的骆驼队在前行
头顶上是白鸽
浪涛中的醉舟在激流而上
深渊中

As the dark of the darkness comes flying in its steps

The fields, deserted, are swallowed by the spreading autumnal wildfire
A group of kids, jumping from history, are on the streets
Cavorting as they kick the sunflowers

Dice, cast, roll into a road
Reaching the foot of the rocks
At dawn, I wake up, as if I had surfaced
From a pond of nothingness

Between the cracks that have appeared in the stone wall
The wind penetrates
People, used to living in the heart of hands
Are exposed on the open sea
The thick smoke, slowly ascending from the bins
Conceals the nomads on the mountain slopes
The people who have climbed to time's scales
Can hold liters of earth in their deep eye-sockets

Poison, mixed with wine
Has time's hands that belong to it
If the clock does not strike in time
The rose petals won't send forth fragrances

Grassland nearby and the sea, in a distance
The camel train, about to dream till it is broken, is moving ahead
Below the white pigeons
A drunken boat, amidst the waves, is upping against the torrent
In the abyss

心灵涌向漩涡

我们围坐时间的火取暖
秃鹰们围绕我们的天空盘旋
林中的空地上两只松鼠
在那一只果实出气
有时昂起头来
向阴影笼罩的树林张望

把迷雾当作盾牌走来的日子
沿着谎言之路行军
一身黑衣的人，不等红灯的熄灭
鲁莽地闯马路走了过去

有人把河底拣到的卵石
扔到了远处
地平线外的尘土报一声回荡
我在空荡无声的房间
玩纸飞机
倾听心中的鼓声
梦中父亲随手关门出去了

从火星传过来的照片上
有人在冲浪
手掌心中集结的台风在
加速
谁把自己想象成孩童
黑板上的词便是
阳光中的蝴蝶

街上走过来两个人

And the heart is surging towards the vortex

We sit in a circle for warmth around time
Bald eagles encircling in our skies
In the clearing, two squirrels
Occasionally raising their heads
Peek at the forest shrouded in the shadows

Days that come walking, with fog as their shield
March along the path of lies
The guy in black, without waiting for the red lights to change
Brashly storms across the road

Someone picks up a pebble from the bottom of the river
And casts it afar
The dust echoes outside the horizon
I, in the silent, empty room
Am playing with paper planes
Listening to the drums inside my heart
My father, in his dream, shuts the door and goes out

In the photographs sent from Mars
Someone is surfing
A typhoon, gathering in the heart of hands
Speeds up
Whoever imagines himself a kid
The words on the blackboard will be
Butterflies in the sunlight

Two people come walking on the street

一个变 成了影子
低飞的乌鸦向憔悴的森林飞去
处在阴蔽和空虚中的我
敲响了严冬

追风筝的孩子们
遇到了多雨的季节
黑夜出远行的人
走上舞台
台上出现的是哈姆雷特

头顶上灯在摇晃
我也在的摇晃
黑森林突如其来的风
开始震怒
滑过冰面的笔尖上
刮起旋风
抬头，灰月亮悠悠地落下

被黑夜牵着离开的群星
不笑，不哭
从墙上的油画落下的油墨
像一张苍白的脸
但比黄昏时的阴影更加变浓

心不断地击鼓，听
是否有人在敲门
雪花突然飘落下来
希望，于无声处
街灯静静熄灭

One turned into a shadow

The crows are flying towards the haggard forest

I, situated in the shade and the vacuity

Knock on the severe winter till it sounds


Kids, chasing after the kites

Have encountered a rainy season

The man who takes a long journey on a dark night

Walks onto the stage

Where Hamlet appears


A lamp is shaking above my head

And I, too, am shaking

The wind that comes sudden in the black forest

Is beginning to rage

The tip of the pen slipping across the ice

Stirs up a whirlwind

When I raise my head, the ashen moon is falling, in a leisurely manner


Stars, led away, by the hand, by the dark night

Neither smile nor cry

The ink, fallen from the oil painting on the wall

Like a pale face

Is denser than the shadows at dusk


The heart keeps drumming. Listen

And see if there's anyone knocking on the door

The snow falls suddenly, fluttering

Hope, in the soundless

The streetlamps, quietly, go out

II

波涛不断侵袭山峰
刺穿出海面的忧虑
是封闭在盲眼中的黑暗

## II

The waves constantly attack the mountain peaks
Worries, poking through the surface of the sea
Are the darkness sealed in the blind eye

# 剧场

舞台
角色窥视自己
寂静愤怒

喧哗
终于浮出水面
序幕被拉开

光与暗
舞台
面具的双脸

观众席一行一行
舞台沉思
导演的灵魂在空中漂浮

剑从手中脱落
几个世纪前的喧哗声
时间被锁定在舞台上

有人把蛋旋转
生活和艺术在较劲
灯熄，留下的是孤独的舞台

台上演员互换角色
风和叶
灵魂寻找自己的回归处

# The Theatre

On the stage
A character steals a look at himself
In silent fury

The commotion
Ends up coming to the surface
As the prelude opens itself

Light and dark
The stage
The double-face of a mask

Rows of audience
The stage in meditation
Where the director's soul is drifting in the air

The sword that slips out of the hand
The commotion from centuries ago
And time, locked on the stage

Someone is turning an egg around
As life and art are in rivalry
When the light goes out, what remains is a solitary stage

Where the actors swap roles
Wind and leaves
While souls are seeking where to return themselves

手持蜡烛的人们派成无尽的路
舞台突然惊醒
跌进水池的雨滴无言无踪

幕后响起脚步声
戴着面具的观众在喧哗
纸上的字迹在燃烧

风息，无声
回忆中观众在舞台上起舞
光和阴悄然合一

演员手持颅骨
生活无话可说
有人在公共汽车上等待下车

舞台屏息
玫瑰刺伤手指
雕像以太阳的足迹变换角度

石头与现实
舞台无门
梦者有一把钥匙

城市在暴雨下狂躁
路上的车分开雨水滑过
有人在台上打着雨伞

舞台上，笼子与鸟
剧作家在思考剧本的最后一幕

Those, candle in hand, are forming endless roads
When the stage suddenly wakes up
And the raindrops that fall into the pond are wordless and traceless

Sound of the footsteps behind the stage
And noise of the audience wearing the masks
The traces of words on paper are burning

Wind extinguished, soundless
In memory, the audience are dancing on the stage
While *ti* and *me* are secretly merging into one

An actor is holding a skull in his hand
Life has nothing to say
Someone is waiting to disembark from a bus

The stage is holding its breath
The rose pricking a finger
The statue changing its angles following the footprints of the sun

Stone and reality
The stage without a door
The dreamer with a single key

The city agitating under a storm
The traffic on the road slipping past, dividing the rain
Someone is holding an umbrella on the stage

Where the cage and the bird
And the playwright is thinking of the last scene in the play

乘客们集在站台避雨

权利的灯在街上一闪一息
洞穴中有进去的足迹，却无出来的
黑暗中剧场在沉思

导演面对着一群演员
花蝴蝶的标本在框框中
静与动

心灵的地平线上升起一片云
剧院与花园
可感应到一阵暴雨的气息

直升机飞过穹顶
掠过的捕食者影子似的
逼害者与屠夫成对地鞠躬

双重命运
演员死在舞台
却活在观众的目中

世纪在碰撞
威武的众神们无表情
鼓掌声中响起孩童的哭叫声

囚徒蹲在圈中
阴影
演出后导演在给观众留签名

While the passengers are gathering on the platform to dodge the rain

The lamps of power on the streets are on and off
There are footprints that go into the cave but none out of it
The stage is in meditation in the darkness

The director is facing a group of actors
Butterfly specimens inside the frames
Stillness and movement

A cloud rises on the horizon of heart
Theatre and garden
Where one can feel the smell of a storm

A helicopter is flying over the dome
Its fleeting shadow like that of a predator
Victims and butchers bowing in pairs

A double-fate
The actors die on the stage
But live in the hearts of the audience

Centuries are colliding
The majestic gods are expressionless
Amidst the rising applause, the cries of the kids

Prisoners squatting in a circle
Shadows
And after the performance, the director is signing autographs for his audience

寒冷刺骨
白雾中朦胧的唯一黑
观众从剧院散尽

墙后响起鼓声
导演的愤怒被演员们团团围住
剧场无人

伪善者撕破自己的脸
人生好似静静的激流中远去的河流
台上演员们不哭，不笑

Piercingly cold

The only blurry blackness in the white fog

The audience have all left the theatre


The sound of drums rises from behind the wall

The fury of the director is encircled by the actors

The theatre is emptied of people


The hypocrite tears off his own face

Life resembles a river that flows far in the quiet torrents

And, on the stage, the actors don't cry, and they don't smile, either

# 选译自《林园》
## 后现代战争时的沉思录

"一个没有历史的民族，
从时间中得不到拯救， 因为历史是一个无始无终之时刻的图案"

      T·S·艾略特 《四个四重奏（小吉丁）》

I

你，回响梦中吞食你自己
把岩石和孤独留在黑暗中
我也是岩石
喧哗声占据天空
我却在虚无的岛屿上
眺望沉默的海
史册的森林被微风吹翻
爆出的击鼓声千年不断
平静的屋檐下灵魂已做好准备
可是内心深处却被纯粹的寒冷麻木
饥饿的词语沾满墙壁
变成巨兽
缓慢地登上意志的祭坛
地图中升起巨大，赤裸裸太阳
东方卷起一场凶猛的万丈风暴
从时间滴下的一株沙粒
在希罗多德＊和史马迁＊的河流中不断地流淌

---

＊ 历史人名。

# *From* Garden of Trees:
# Meditations on the Postmodern Wars

*A people without history*
*Is not redeemed from time, for history is a pattern*
*Of timeless moments.*
> T. E. Eliot ('Little Gidding', *The Four Quartets*)

I

You, remembering how you swallow yourself up in a dream
Have left the rock and loneliness in the darkness
I, too, am a rock
While the commotion fills the skies
I stay on an island of nihility
Watching the silent ocean
A forest, of the annals of history, is turned over with the blow of a breeze
As the explosive sound of drumming is continuous for thousands of years
Under a quiet roof, the soul has been prepared
Although it is numbed by the purity of coldness in the depths of heart
Hungry words, pasted all over the wall
Are turning into huge animals
As they slowly ascend to the altar of will
An enormous naked sun is rising on the map
As a storm, fierce and thousands of meters long, is whirling up in the East
A stem of sand, dripping from time
Keeps flowing in the river of
Herodotus and Sima Qian

滚滚乌云万变中出现的神奇的脸
那面孔上蛛网般的皱纹就是你

无形锁链似的小路奔向草原
一声骰响，被弓玄亲吻的矢飞向自己的目标
手掌心便是那令人目眩的路的尽头
焕发出虹彩的盾牌诱惑着马背上人
命运的曲线在盲点上交叉
瞰欲谷＊翁的碑独自留在无言的沙丘中
赛种人＊＊头盔上绝伦的羽毛在夕阳余辉下宝石般闪烁

一滴血，太阳
燃烧的紫罗兰潜逃似地掠过苍穹
也落进我眼珠黑色的大洋中
在新的广场上
近处的榆林随阴风恼怒飘然
夜，临近的黑暗，另一个震颤的海
被砍下的头颅在一个装满血的皮袋中冲着
夜，　茫茫沙丘
波涛在陶瓮中瀑晓
一切伤口铭刻在稳弊的石头中

―――――――

＊　　历史人名。
＊＊　公元前生活在中亚的游牧名族的名称。

78

The magical face that appears in the changing clouds
With a cobweb of wrinkles is you


A path, like a shapeless chain, is rushing towards the grassland
And, with a knocking sound, an arrow, kissed by the bowstring, flies
                                                           towards its own target
The heart of the hand being the end of the dazzling path
The rainbow of a shield seducing the figure on horseback
The curves of destination intersect on the blind spot
With Tonyu Kuk's gravestone left alone, in the wordless sand-dunes
The unique plumes, on the helmets of thescythians, twinkling like gems in
                                                           the after-glow


A drop of blood, the sun
The burning violets sweeping cross the firmament as if running away
While falling into the black ocean of my eyeballs
On the new square
The elm trees, nearby, are floating, getting angry with the cold wind
Night, the approaching darkness, another shivering ocean
A head, beheaded, is being flushed in a leather bag, full of blood
Night, vast sand-dunes
Waves are roaring in the porcelain urn
All the wounds carved inside the steady stone

II

堕落的旧围墙突然倒塌
中心花园变成深沉的广场
腐朽的铁链杆间
晒到绿草地的一缕柔光
也在变
幽林中的小道
以消失在旧花园的记忆中
篱笆上散漫的犹豫
欲动翅膀的瓢虫也飞走了
我一时迷失了方向
太阳的利剑把一切切割成
黑与白的世界
杂草丛生的旷野又枯又绿，难舍难分
泥土深处的蚯蚓为了躲避
太阳那无情的毒箭
在等待着黑暗，等待着长夜
等待着雨水和寒冷
高傲的狂风在古老的史剧中扫膛街头
飞过湖面的天鹅如传说
穿过古钱币细嫩的铜心
盲人手中探路的拐杖声
掀起一片震响，慢慢破裂的命运
千秋拥挤的时间峡谷干涸
留下的是几滴血迹
如此地鲜艳
台阶到台阶便是手挽手的沉默
阴郁，迷惘，怀疑的步伐
我想到了那些痛苦的冤魂

II

The corrupt old wall collapsed on a sudden

As the central garden turned into a profound square

And between the rotten ironchains

A ray of soft light that went through to shed on the green lawn

Was also changing

The path in the quiet woods

Has disappeared in the old garden's memory

With the discursive hesitation on the fence

The ladybug, whose wings were about to stir, has now flown away

Temporarily, I have lost my direction

When the sword of the sun cut everything into a world

Of black and white

The wilderness, overgrown with weeds, is a mixture of withered greenness

The worms, in the depths of the soil and to escape

From the ruthless poisoned arrows of the sun

Are waiting for the darkness, for the long nights

And for the rain and coldness

The arrogant squall is sweeping the streets, in an ancient historical play

The swans that are flying across the lake are like in a legend

Going through the tender copper-heart of the ancient coin

The sound of the walking-stick as the blindman uses it in search of a road

Stirs up a roaring sound, and in the slowly fragmenting fate

The valley of time, crowded with thousands of autumns, has dried up

Leaving traces of a few drops of blood

So bright-coloured

That there is silence hand in hand from one flight of steps to another

With gloomy, confused and doubtful steps

I happen to think of those painful ghosts of the wronged

临阵的朝霞中露珠在青草尖闪烁
仿佛是寒酸的泪滴
是的，一只蚯蚓倦缩在大理石台阶上
阴影渴望着光线
呼吸着早晨的清香，脚踏大理石台阶的我
也在沉湎于酣梦中

In the morning glow on the battleground, pearls of dew are shining on the
tips of green grass
Like shabby teardrops
Yes, a worm, curling up in the shadow
Of a marble step, hankering after the light
Breathing in the fragrance of the morning while I, stepping up the marble
steps
Am also immersed in a sound dream

IV

无比的高处垂落
掉进深渊中…
是谁的双掌成上我
纯洁的预言声中等待我…

锁住世界的窗玻璃被打碎
狂妄的喧哗声马群似的闯进屋内
街上的破烂碎纸随风飘浮
头顶上摇晃的灯光是我变为
无数的阴影，撞击记忆
从中有人乱了阵脚
小鸟急速地飞入窗前的一棵榆树墩中去
黑暗一片哗然
沉重的铁门一声巨响下关闭
黑色的洞穴内传出昨日的尖叫

凌乱的黑暗涌进我的心
陌生的海锁定萎缩的岛
绝妙的赞美声照亮雪地的边缘
深渊到深渊…. 我在哭泣

打开窗户把书扔出去
从手掌心飞出的是惊恐的群鸽
翅膀无意地拍打，述说
战斧式导弹的轰鸣声中
幽幽响起莫扎特的临终曲
漆黑的天空飘下一滴滴亮晶晶血
大地一声震响

IV

The infinite height has fallen
Into the abyss...
Who is it whose palms offer me
And who is waiting for me in the purity of a prophesy...

The windowpane that has locked up the world has been shattered
Presumptuous commotion, like a pack of horses, is storming into my house
Rubbish and broken pieces of paper, on the street, are floating in the wind
The lamplight that is swaying above me is the countless shadows
That I have turned into, hitting against memory
Someone is left in disarray
A little bird rapidly flies into the elm stump outside the window
Darkness in an uproar
The heavy iron-door closes, with a huge sound
Shriekings of yesterday are now coming out of the dark cave

Chaotic darkness is rushing into my heart
As the strange sea is putting the shrunken island under lock and key
Perfect praise is shining on the edge of the snow
From an abyss to another...I'm crying

When I open the window to throw the books out
It is the frightened doves that fly out of my palm
Their wings fluttering and talking, meaninglessly
And, in the noise of the tomahawk cruise missiles
Faintly rises a terminal melody of Mozart's
A shining drop of blood falls floating out of the pitch-dark skies
And the earth roars

弹奏出的是生命的哀伤
有个小孩在成废墟的街角处向暗处的我挥挥手
她那天使般含泪的笑容
是我内心的森林更加暗淡
像是对我莫名含恨的无比的谴责

我降生第一次喊出声，众生恐惧
天空和大地骚动
天地起浮在一颗豆壳中
我见到的是一个墓穴
在阳光里

从何而来，何处去

Giving forth the sadness of life

A kid is waving at me in the darkness from a street corner in ruins

Her tearful smile, like that of an angel

Makes the forest inside my heart go darker

As if in baffled, hateful and matchless accusation


It's my first cry since I was born, the fearful masses

The skies and the earth, astir

Are fluctuating in a peapod

But all I see is a grave

Under the sun


Where do we come from and where do we go?

V

干渴的河滩中挖出的井
挖出的是卵石，碎石，沙子和饥饿
是过去的时间留下的足迹
是古老史诗吟唱出的最后一行

嘹亮的黑暗升腾的房间
两个人无意中叹息
空气中飘流的海妖歌声
使人沉闷中打盹
隐没于绿草丛中的河
静静流过城市的郊野
月光中拖着孤影的你
双眼遥望星空
沼泽中咚眠的一根灰色草
梦中飞翔
带面具的人走出自己的鸟笼
泥土中的词语敲击琴弦
被敲击的是完整的世界
还未诞生的小鸟
心灵的震响中迅速变老
陶醉至极的嫩枝过早地
被春天的暴风雨所止断
暴涨的河流无言的激情中
跟进沙漠的浪尖
夜莺的歌声惬意地解释着
刻在水面上的词
失声涕泣的马头琴以爆出
硫黄酸的味道

V


The well, dug out of the parched floodplain

Shows the diggings to be pebbles, gravels, sands and hunger

Traces left by time in the past

The last line chanted out of an ancient epic


In the sonorous room in which the darkness is rising

The two are sighing without realizing they are doing it

The song of siren, adrift in the air

Causes one to nod away, bored

And the river, hidden in the clusters of green grass

Is quietly running through the wild suburbia of the city

You, dragging a lonely shadow in the moonlight

Raise your eyes to look at the starry skies

A blade of grey grass, hibernating in the swamp

Is flying in a dream

While the man, wearing a mask, is walking out of his own birdcage

Words, in the soil, are knocking on the strings

But what is being knocked at is the totality of a world

A little bird, not yet born

Fast ages in the vibration of the heart

The intoxicated tender branch has been broken

By the spring storm before its time

In the wordless passion of the surging river

The tips of the waves in the desert are following up

Songs of a nightingale explain, with pleasure

The words carved on the surface of the water

A horse-head stringed instrument, sobbing uncontrollably, is sending forth

The smell of sulfuric acid

寂寞的墙壁空无
昨日的时间惶逃中丢失
一面镜子
飘荡的幻影不见了
留下的是苍白的赤裸
油画像月色充溢的果园
如同白，绿，黄，红…… 黑
参合出大千世界的形状
正午的阳光下
昨天的时间和今天的时间停留在画中
镜中人走进缭绕的烟雾
无数碎镜片中纷飞的来日
在阴影里思索自己的无奈
悠扬而淡远的古老诗篇终于被吟唱出来
在诗篇的最后一行窥视你

The solitary walls remain empty

A mirror was lost

In the hurried escape of time yesterday

Drifting apparitions are gone

Leaving behind a pale nakedness

A painting is like a garden, filled with moonlight

In white, green, yellow, red,...and black

Merging into the shapes of a great world

Under the noon sunlight

Yesterday's time and today's time are stopped in the painting

People in the mirror are walking into the curling smoke

Coming days are flying about in the countless broken pieces of the mirror

Thinking of their own helplessness in the shadow

The ancient poem, melodious and remote, has finally managed to be sung

Peeping at you out of the last line of the poem

X

夜，一张空洞的网
掀起最初的细光
黑暗中开始出现裂缝
巢穴中的蛋却紧闭的无缝
夜莺的歌声越不出自己的鸟笼
光和阴在时间的静点盘旋

茶杯放在桌子上已久
早已热散暖尽
老人触摸墓碑
无法跳脱淡淡的稳寐
彩色绝伦的玫瑰芬芳中
凋谢，哭泣
粗糙的树根似的手指感受
唤醒死神的文字
月光下蒙着一层银色面纱的墓地
寂寞中抵缺遗忘
猫头鹰的低鸣声好似
婴儿的哭泣声
融化在昏暗寂静中的你
拿起茶杯
从没被说出过得孤独围绕着心
心灵与想象的赤裸陪伴你

谁的手在宁转门上的钥匙
草原的梦在延续
是风和海啸的激情
一时无声

X

Night, a hollow and empty net
Is lifting the first fine light
Darkness begins to show fissures
Although the eggs in the nests are seamlessly closed
The song of a nightingale can't go beyond its own cage
Ti/me and t/i'm/e are encircling around the quiescent point of time

The teacup has been placed on the table for a long time
Its heat long gone
The old man touches the gravestone
But he can't jump off the faint steady sleep
In the fragrant roses, colorful beyond comparison
That are shedding, and weeping
Fingers, like rough roots, are feeling
For the words of Death, trying to wake them up
The graveyard is shrouded in a silvery veil under the moon
Reaching oblivion in solitude
The low hooting of an owl sounds
Like the crying of a baby
You, having melted in the dim quiet
Are picking up the teacup
A sense of loneliness, never voiced, encircling the heart
Soul and imagination keeping you company

Whose hands are turning the key in the door
The dream is continuing on the grassland
It is the passion of wind and tsunami
That goes quiet

却有回来了
是群马逼进时震撼大地的铁蹄声
你在倾听，钥匙在转
门外开始出现朝霞


清晨
过去的时间和现在的时间
涌入广场
别以为天鹅的临终绝唱是 *
无奈的抵抗
那是鸣警
（我不想死抱徒劳的期待）
阴影和阳光的混沌中
那显露出来的脸
面对着铁窗而入的海风沉思
游戏中的孩子们在
按自己的规则玩耍
耳中不断地响起
来自遥远的幽笛声
狱中，面对淡淡夕阳的老人
为来日的清晨默念
脸上的皱纹比平时更加深沉
挂在墙壁的马头琴变天鹅
拍打翅膀

---

* 苏格拉底，西方式民主的最有名的拥护者和牺牲品。在谈话中，苏格拉底把自己的死等同于天鹅的临终绝唱，这正是他临终时形象的传神写照，他说，在我看来，这些鸟儿也好，天鹅也好，都不是因为悲哀而歌唱。它们歌唱是因为知道在那个不可见的世界有好东西在等着它们，那一天它们会比从前更加快乐。苏格拉底就是这样，平静而快乐地迎接了自己的死亡。一代圣哲苏格拉底的伟大形象，依靠弟子柏拉图的生花妙笔，就这样流传了下来。

But comes back again

It's the ironclad hooves shaking the earth when the horses are getting closer

You are listening and the key is turning

Dawn is showing up outside the door


Early morning

Time of the past and time of the present

Are rushing into the square

Don't assume that the swansong*

Is helpless resistance

But it's a warning

(I don't cling to vain expectations)

In the mixture of shadows and sunshine

The face that is revealed

Is thinking in the face of the sea wind that comes into the window

Kids in play are

Playing by their own rules

A faint flute from afar

Keeps ringing in the ears

In the prison, an old man, facing the faint setting sun

Is meditating for the coming day

The wrinkles on his face deeper than normal

The horse-head stringed instrument, hanging from the wall, has turned into a swan

Fluttering its wings

---

\* Socrates, the most well-known of the supporters and victims of Western democracy...
In a conversation, Socrates regarded his own death as a 'swansong', which is a vivid
portraiture of his own image at death. He said, 'To me, the birds or the swans do not sing
because they are sad...they sing because they know there are good things waiting for
them in an invisible world and that they'll be happier when that day comes.' Thus Socrates
welcomed his own death in a peaceful and happy manner. That is how the great image of
Socrates, a saintly philosopher, is carried on by his disciple Plato with his wonderful pen.

涌入草原的无数条路
究竟走向何方？
拖着阴影的夜中
飞出一对燕子和猫头鹰
有人在广场等待
来日的到来
被时间刺穿的过去
钉在今天
恐惧
把一块冰糖放进清茶中
溶化
紧闭成石头的时间
发出的箭：
昨日哭喊的孩童
今天喊出尖叫声

Countless paths that rush into the grassland

Where on earth are they going?

Out of the night dragging its shadows

A pair of swallows and an owl have flown

Someone is waiting on the square

For the coming day to arrive

The past, pierced by time

Is nailed on today

While fear

Puts a rock candy in a cup of clear tea

To melt

The arrow shot by time

That has closed into a stone:

The kids who were crying yesterday

Are now shrieking today

XI

此时，此刻，不知不觉中
你开始奔跑
奔跑中消失
薄雾笼罩桥头
响起脚踏声
凝视流淌的河水，默念
空无中沉淀出一片寂静
一滴阴影在挣脱
悲哀声中没入自己的绝境

是我
岸边沙滩上，脚迈着碎浪
蜡烛的暗处走出一条路
暴风雨夜打着黑伞走过去的
是我

一棵树在回忆
森林深处传来的心跳声中
啄木鸟琢磨靶心
凛凛的树叶和绿草丛尖
停留的光在起帆
暮色中摸索窗玻璃的残光
摸出的是黑森林中的轻雾和小路
江河以平静中流过旱旱的草原
街拐出有人躲闪着脸额
并望出不详的一眼
沼泽中露出的脚印，心头中的阴影
被僵尸般的黑夜拖了进去

XI

Here and now, without knowing it
You begin running
To disappear in the running
A thin fog shrouds the bridgehead
The sound of steps falling
Gazing at the running river waters, murmuring in silence
A vastness of quiet, deposited from nothing
A drop of shadow is struggling
Sinking into its own impasse in the sound of sadness

It's me
On the beach by the bank, the feet stepping onto the broken waves
A road walks out of the darkness of a candle
It is I who walked past, holding a black umbrella
On a stormy night

A tree is remembering
In the heart-leaping that comes from the depths of the forest
A woodpecker is grinding the bull's eye
The light, stopped among the stern leaves and blades of green grass
Is setting sail
The residual light that is groping for the windowpane at dusk
Touches instead the light fog of the black forest and the path
Rivers quietly run across the grassland in an early drought
Someone is dodging with his face around the corner of a street
And throws an ominous glance
Footsteps revealed in a swamp, and shadows in the heart
Are dragged in by the corpse-like night

结霜的街道被镜片挡在外面
归入石头中的夜以厌倦追捕者的贪婪

指挥棒沿历史的足迹挥舞
无意间穿透
演奏者前摆正好的曲谱
蛛网在过滤时间
大理石雕刻出的巨人
脸色苍白
苍白的表情如绝望
禽在蜂酶中的蜜蜂在挣扎
随风飘扬的花粉以张开翅膀
两条江河灰暗的浪涛中流向北方的大海
原野，灵魂如奔驰的骏马
无形的烈火越过奔腾的河床
封闭在岩石中的苍狼
古人头顶上高高升起的
明月中孔叫
草原，神圣的忍耐
口中含出无名酸涩
是一捏泥土的滋味

走完　根到绿叶的　一生
高傲的浮影　悬挂在树枝上
畅饮长风　爬上云叶　飘然离去

The frosty streets are kept outside by the lens

The night, returned to the stone, has grown tired of the pursuer's greed


The baton is being brandished along the traces of history

And accidentally pierces

The music score, placed right in front of the performer

The spider's web is filtering time

And the giant, carved on the granite

Looks pale

So desperately pale

A bee, caught in the honey, is struggling

Pollens, aflutter in the wind, are spreading their wings open

The dim grey waves of the two rivers are flowing into the northern sea

The plain, its soul like a galloping horse

The fire, shapeless, is crossing the rushing riverbed

The gray wolf, concealed in the rock

Is yelling to the moon

That rose high above the heads of the ancient people

The grassland, sacred endurance

Sour austerity in the mouth

A pinch of soil


Finishing    a whole life    from roots to leaves

The arrogant floating shadows    hanging from the branches

Taking a deep drink of a long wind    to climb the cloud-leaf    and drift away